AMY STERLING CASIL

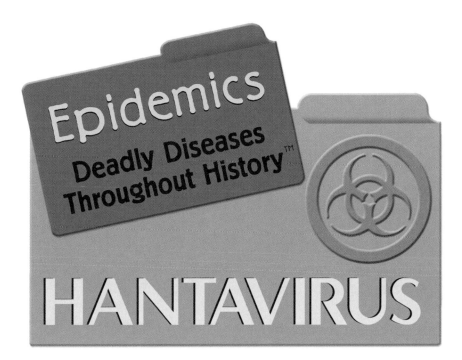

Epidemics
Deadly Diseases
Throughout History™

HANTAVIRUS

The Rosen Publishing Group, Inc.
New York

Published in 2005 by The Rosen Publishing Group, Inc.
29 East 21st Street, New York, NY 10010

Library of Congress Cataloging-in-Publication Data

Casil, Amy Sterling.
Hantavirus/by Amy Sterling Casil.—1st ed.
    p. cm.—(Epidemics)
Includes bibliographical references and index.
ISBN 1-4042-0254-4 (library binding)
1. Hantavirus infections—Epidemiology—Juvenile literature.
I. Title. II. Series.
RA644.H32C37 2005
616.9′18—dc22

                                      2004013897

Manufactured in the United States of America

On the cover: Electron microscope image of the Sin Nombre virus, which causes hantavirus pulmonary syndrome

CONTENTS

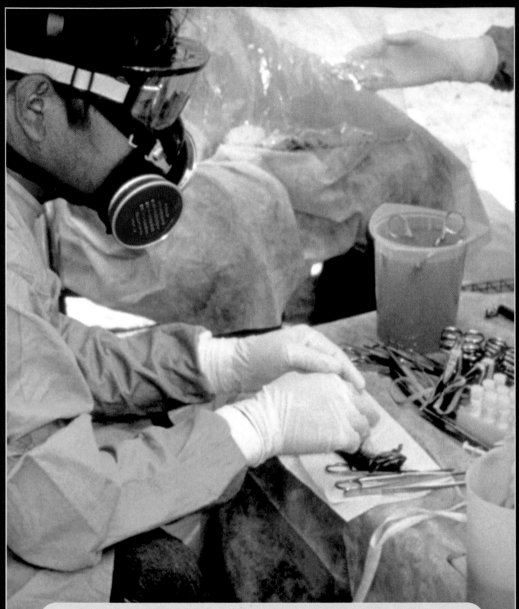

A Centers for Disease Control and Prevention (CDC) scientist collects specimens from trapped rodents during the 1993 hantavirus epidemic in the southwestern United States.

INTRODUCTION

The Four Corners area of the southwestern United States is where the states of Arizona, New Mexico, Colorado, and Utah all meet. At this intersection, the states' borders create four right-angled corners, and it is possible for a visitor to straddle the corners and have his or her hands and feet in four different states simultaneously. But the Four Corners area is not only a tourist novelty. As the ancestral home of the Navajo people, it is also very rich in history and Native American tradition. In May 1993, however, this beautiful and fascinating region became shadowed by a mysterious and often fatal pulmonary (lung) illness.

First, a young, very fit Navajo man was rushed to a New Mexico hospital, complaining of breathing problems. Within hours, he was dead. Puzzled hospital workers, trying to understand the tragedy, were astonished to find that he had been on his way to his fiancée's funeral when he was stricken. She had died a few days earlier, after suffering similar symptoms.

The young couple's tragic deaths provided the clue to the discovery of what would turn out to be an ancient and deadly virus. Dr. James Cheek of the Indian Health Service (IHS) said, "I think if it hadn't been for that initial pair of people that became sick within a week of each other, we never would have discovered the illness at all," as quoted on the CDC's "All About Hantaviruses" Web page. A silent killer was stalking the Four Corners area, and the race was on to discover its cause and put an end to it.

1

THE DISCOVERY OF THE SIN NOMBRE VIRUS

Following the sudden deaths of the Navajo couple, the New Mexico Office of Medical Investigations launched an investigation to discover if there had been any other similar illnesses in the Four Corners area. Dr. Bruce Tempest of the IHS discovered five other recent cases of young, healthy people who had died suddenly of respiratory failure. Intensive tests showed that the illness was not a previously known disease, such as bubonic plague.

Uncertain about what they were dealing with, New Mexico authorities notified the Centers for Disease Control and Prevention (CDC), the lead federal agency charged with protecting the health and safety of Americans at home and abroad. The CDC handed the case over to its Special Pathogens

Branch, which is the division responsible for outbreaks of highly dangerous and new diseases. Working together, the CDC, the Indian Health Service, the Navajo nation, the University of New Mexico, and the state health departments of New Mexico, Colorado, and Utah swung into action to combat the mysterious disease. This outbreak was especially terrifying because 70 percent of the people who were initially infected with the virus died, making the new disease an ultradangerous CDC level 4 infectious agent.

The CDC quickly performed genetic testing on tissue samples from the Four Corners victims in order to eliminate other possible causes of death such as pesticide poisoning or a bacterial infection. When the test results came back, CDC researchers were able to narrow down the possibilities. They discovered that the virus that had caused the infection was a type of hantavirus, an agent of infection that had first been scientifically observed among U.S. soldiers in the Korean War (1950–1953). The disease-causing virus was named after the Hantaan River in Korea, and its name was shortened to "hantavirus."

Finding the Culprit

Researchers knew that all previously discovered hantaviruses had been transmitted by rodents, mostly mice and rats. Throughout the summer of 1993, investigators from all of the cooperating federal, state, and local government health agencies trapped rodents inside and outside homes where people who had hantavirus infections had lived, as well as in piñon (southwestern pine) groves and summer sheep camps where some of the victims had worked. Additional rodents were trapped for comparison in and around nearby unaffected households.

In seeking to identify the disease quickly, researchers nevertheless had to remain sensitive to the feelings of local people. All previous outbreaks of hantavirus had been transmitted by rodents, so researchers risked their own health when they started to trap these animals without wearing full infectious-disease protective gear, which resembles a space suit. "We didn't want to go in wearing respirators, scaring . . . everybody," John Sarisky, an Indian Health Service environmental disease specialist, says on the Centers for Disease Control hantavirus Web page. Dressed in ordinary street clothes, the researchers trapped nearly 1,700 rodents of all types in the targeted areas. Later, when the animals were dissected and tested in CDC labs and other labs, scientists wore protective gear, including gloves, gowns, and respirators.

Out of the many different kinds of rodents that were trapped, CDC investigators discovered that the deer mouse (scientific name *Peromyscus maniculatus*) was the animal that was carrying a previously undiscovered kind of hantavirus. The deer mouse lived in rural and semirural areas, mostly near human habitations—in woodpiles and barns and inside people's homes. Because deer mice lived in the affected area and because they were carrying the new strain of hantavirus, researchers strongly suspected that they were the carrier of the disease that had killed the young, healthy victims in the Four Corners area.

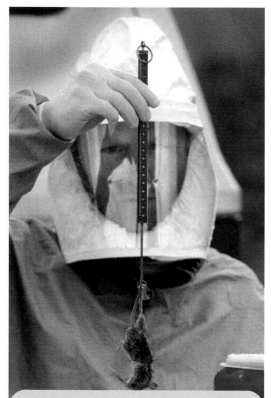

A University of New Mexico researcher examines a mouse caught in a 1996 hantavirus study that took place in Placitas, New Mexico.

Researchers then took the next step in their scientific detective work: a case investigation. They compared the "case" households of people who had gotten the disease with nearby "control" households of those unaffected by hantavirus. Control households were similar in most respects to those where the case patients lived, except that no one who lived in the control households had gotten the disease.

Investigators found and trapped more rodents in case households than in control households. From this they learned that more rodents had been living in close contact with people in the case households. Second, they learned that people in case households were more likely than those in control households to do cleaning around the house or outdoor work in fields or gardens. They still did not know if the risk for contracting hantavirus came from performing these tasks or from entering closed-up, poorly ventilated rooms or closets to get gardening tools or cleaning supplies.

By November 1993, this scientific detective work began to pay off: the CDC Special Pathogens Branch grew the newly discovered form of hantavirus from the tissue of a deer mouse that had been trapped near one of the homes of a person who had gotten the disease. Separately, the U.S. Army Medical Research Institute of Infectious Diseases (USAMRIID) also grew the same virus from tissues taken from a New Mexico victim and from the tissues of a mouse that had been trapped in California.

Sin Nombre Virus

From summer to fall 1993, many doctors, scientists, and other health professionals worked together to trace the source of the deadly outbreak and isolate the cause. The new form of hantavirus was first named Muerto Canyon virus, after the place where it was first found in the Four Corners area. "Muerto" means "death" in Spanish. Although this name for the virus seemed chillingly accurate, it was also disturbing and offensive to the Navajo and Spanish-speaking people who lived in the area. Researchers quickly changed the new virus's name to Sin Nombre virus or SNV. Sin Nombre means "without a name" or "no name" in Spanish. SNV is still the name for this virus today. The potentially fatal disease syndrome caused by the virus was named hantavirus pulmonary syndrome, or HPS. It remains the deadliest result of hantavirus infection.

As the CDC notes, the rapid identification and isolation of SNV was a triumph of interagency cooperation. It was also an important milestone in the continuing development of modern tests for viruses. The Sin Nombre strain of hantavirus was discovered in only a few months. In contrast, it took several decades for the first strain of hantavirus, the Korean Hantaan strain, to be discovered and isolated.

One of the reasons why researchers were able to identify the Sin Nombre virus so quickly and to differentiate it from other strains of hantavirus was their use of a laboratory technique called polymerase chain reaction (PCR). PCR is a common method of creating billions of copies of specific fragments of a virus's DNA. Researchers then compare these copies of viral DNA with the DNA of other viruses to determine how they are related, if at all.

Researchers developed a test that used PCR in order to detect the differences between the Sin Nombre hantavirus strain and other hantaviruses that had been previously discovered. This helped them understand what kind of disease they were dealing with, how it was spread, how it should be treated, and how new infections could be prevented. More recently, scientists at the CDC used a PCR-based test to isolate and discover the coronavirus that caused the severe acute respiratory syndrome (SARS) outbreak that began in Guangdong Province, China, in 2003. Coronaviruses are extremely common in humans and animals. Usually the most severe disease symptoms they cause are coldlike complaints, but SARS was a far more deadly infection, killing more than 700 people worldwide in 2003.

Scientific advances like PCR combined with cooperation between local, state, and national health organizations, as well as with the research laboratories of the nation's colleges and universities, helped to make the 1993 identification of the Sin Nombre strain of hantavirus one of the quickest on record.

Ancient Virus, Ancient Wisdom

In the course of their research, scientists also learned that the 1993 outbreak was not the first time people had been infected with hantavirus in the southwestern United States. As part of their study, CDC scientists examined tissue from people who had died of unexplained lung illnesses in the past. Through this detective work, they discovered that the earliest known case of confirmed HPS was found in the lungs of a Utah man who had died in 1959.

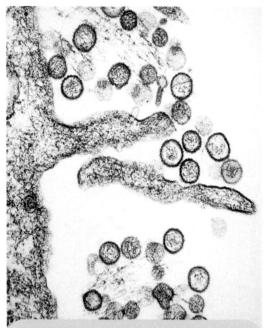

This is an electron micrograph of the Sin Nombre virus taken by the CDC, which continues to study the virus.

Other studies and local Four Corners–area scientists discovered that although HPS had been previously unknown to Western medical researchers, Navajo traditions referred to a very similar illness that was often associated with mice. Some Navajo healers even predicted the 1993 outbreak because their traditions told them that in years of increased rainfall, mouse populations increased, thus causing greater risk of the disease. Ecology had indeed played a role in the 1993 outbreak, as the Navajo healers had predicted it would. Scientists found that mouse and rat populations had increased dramatically following the wet winter caused by the El Niño weather phenomenon in the Pacific Ocean. An El Niño weather pattern refers to unusually warm surface ocean temperatures caused by a slackening of the trade winds. This rise in ocean temperatures usually leads to a rise in rainfall in parts of the western United States.

Interestingly, the Navajo recommendations for prevention of the disease exactly matched those of twentieth-century scientists, including, most important of all, the avoidance of contact with rodents and their waste. In addition, Navajo awareness of the disease even predated the first appearance of bubonic plague (another fatal, rodent-borne illness) in their communities. So, the tragic hantavirus outbreak of 1993 brought an ancient killer to the public's attention and represented a fascinating and rare link between traditional Native American knowledge and the most up-to-date techniques known to modern science.

1952
Nearly 3,000 American soldiers contract an acute hemorrhagic syndrome known by the name of Korean hemorrhagic fever.

1959
A thirty-eight-year-old Utah man develops what will later be identified as the earliest case of hantavirus pulmonary syndrome.

Early 1993
Heavy snows and rainfall in the American Southwest greatly increase the deer mouse food supply, allowing the mice to reproduce rapidly. The swelling deer mice population comes into greater contact with humans.

May 1993
An outbreak of an unexplained pulmonary illness occurs in a region of the southwestern United States known as the Four Corners. A young, physically fit Navajo man suffering from shortness of breath is rushed to a hospital in New Mexico and dies very rapidly. His fiancée died several days earlier after suffering from similar symptoms.

1978
H. W. Lee discovers the infectious agent of Korean hemorrhagic fever, which he names the Hantaan virus after a river located on the border between the two Koreas. Soon afterward a very similar virus is isolated in Scandinavia and becomes known as the Puumala virus.

November 1993

The specific hantavirus that caused the Four Corners outbreak is isolated. The new virus is called Muerto Canyon virus—later changed to Sin Nombre virus (SNV)—and the new disease caused by the virus is named hantavirus pulmonary syndrome (HPS).

1996

An outbreak of HPS occurs in Argentina. Since this outbreak, cases of HPS caused by hantaviruses have been documented in Brazil, Canada, Chile, Paraguay, and Uruguay, making HPS a panhemispheric disease.

June 1993

A Louisiana bridge inspector who had not traveled to the Four Corners area develops hantavirus pulmonary syndrome (HPS). An investigation discovers another hantavirus, named the bayou virus, which is carried by the rice rat.

Late 1993

A Florida man who had not traveled to the Four Corners area develops HPS symptoms. As a result, a new hantavirus, the Black Creek Canal virus, is identified. It is spread by cotton rats. A Sin Nombre–like virus is identified in New York City and named New York-1. It is spread by the white-footed mouse.

Summer 1993

An investigation combs the entire Four Corners region to find any other people who have a similar case history. Five more young, healthy people who all died after acute respiratory failure are identified. The CDC joins the investigation. Additional cases are reported, as flu, herbicide exposure, and bubonic plague are ruled out as causes of the illness.

2

OTHER OUTBREAKS OF HANTAVIRUS

Following the 1993 Four Corners outbreak, CDC researchers discovered that the Sin Nombre virus was not the only form of hantavirus that caused HPS, the lung syndrome that is the most deadly effect of hantavirus infection. In the summer of 1993, a Louisiana bridge inspector came down with a fatal case of HPS, but he had not traveled to the Southwest. Testing showed that the virus he had been infected with was similar but not identical to the Sin Nombre strain of the virus. This new virus was called bayou virus, and it was not transmitted by a deer mouse but was instead carried and transmitted by the rice rat *(Oryzomys palustris)*. In late 1993, a thirty-three-year-old Florida man who also had never traveled to the Four Corners area came down with HPS symptoms but later recovered. A similar CDC investigation revealed yet another hantavirus, named the Black Creek Canal virus. Its carrier was found to be the cotton rat *(Sigmodon hispidus)*. Soon after, another case occurred in New York. This time, the Sin Nombre–like virus was named New York-1, and the white-footed mouse, *Peromyscus leucopus*, was identified as the carrier.

Korean Hemorrhagic Fever

The first-identified illness caused by a hantavirus was Korean hemorrhagic fever, which victimized U.S. soldiers during the Korean War in the 1950s. All hantaviruses are hemorrhagic, which means they trigger the leakage of blood from the infected person's capillaries, or small blood vessels.

Between 1951 and 1954 in Korea, 3,200 U.S. soldiers fell ill with a fever that affected their kidney function. Between 5 and 10 percent of the soldiers died. Though this was a different type of disease syndrome from the pulmonary (lung) failure caused by the Sin Nombre virus in the American Southwest, the Korean virus was nevertheless a related strain. Because it was still very difficult for scientists to isolate and test for viruses in the 1950s, the Korean strain of hantavirus was not identified until 1976, when Korean researchers discovered it in the striped field mouse, a rodent common in Korea with the scientific name of *Apodemus agrarius*.

This newly isolated virus was named Hantaan virus after the Hantaan River in Korea, which flowed near the places where U.S. soldiers were stationed and contracted the disease more than twenty years before. The disease caused by the Hantaan strain of hantavirus was called hemorrhagic fever with renal syndrome, or HFRS. Renal syndrome refers to the kidney problems suffered by those infected with the Hantaan virus. A similar disease that was carried by rats was identified in the 1980s and named the Seoul strain, after the capital city of South Korea.

One fascinating but unproven theory concerning the first-identified cases of hantavirus-based illness states that the outbreak among U.S. soldiers in Korea may have been a result of biological warfare. Few people know that Japanese scientists were working on biological, or "germ," warfare during World War II. The special branch of the Japanese military devoted to germ warfare was called Unit 731. Japanese military scientists experimented on Korean, Chinese, and American prisoners of war, infecting them with diseases like bubonic plague and yellow fever.

Following the end of World War II, the American military governor of Japan, General Douglas

MacArthur, employed some of the Unit 731 scientists to develop biological warfare techniques for use in the Korean War. The Unit 731 scientists are thought by some to have experimented with hantavirus, which they knew was transmitted through rats and mice. An unproven but common story among Korean War veterans tells the tale of infected mice and rats being released into North Korea during the first years of the Korean War. It could be merely a coincidence that so many U.S. soldiers were infected with hantavirus after they crossed the 38th Parallel—the geographic line between North and South Korea. But some veterans believe it was no coincidence.

U.S. Army doctors treat a Korean civilian injured during the American bombing of Inchon in 1950.

They are convinced that the Korean hantavirus outbreak was the creation of Japanese germ warfare scientists who went to work for the U.S. military after the Second World War.

Hantaviruses Around the World

Hantavirus exists in one form or another throughout the entire world. Hantaviruses belong to the bunya-virus family of viruses. There are five types of viruses within the family: bunyavirus, phlebovirus, nairovirus, tospovirus, and hantavirus. Before the 1993 Four Corners outbreak, hantavirus-based illnesses were thought to be exclusively confined to the Eastern Hemisphere, partly because the first identified cases were found in Korea. And just as U.S. physicians and scientists discovered that the Navajo people who lived in the Four Corners area had long known about hantavirus-caused illness, Eastern Hemisphere physicians and healers have also been aware of the disease for hundreds of years. However, pre-1993 outbreaks of hantavirus-based illness have been documented in both the Western and the Eastern Hemispheres: Russia in 1913 and 1932, among Japanese troops in Manchuria (a part of China) also in 1932, and in Sweden in 1934.

Researchers Connie Schmaljohn and Brian Hjelle, from the University of New Mexico, report that between 150,000 and 200,000 cases of hantavirus-caused illness occur each year. More than half of these cases are found in China, with many others dis-covered in Korea. Other countries strongly affected by

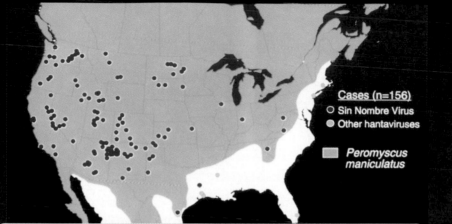

Distribution* of the *Peromyscus maniculatus* and Location of Hantavirus Pulmonary Syndrome Cases, January 27, 1997

Cases (n=156)
○ Sin Nombre Virus
● Other hantaviruses

▨ *Peromyscus maniculatus*

This 1997 CDC map shows the range of the deer mouse (in blue) along with the incidence of hantavirus infection. As this mouse and other virus-carrying rodents are so widespread, the only way to protect against infection is through sanitation and effective medicines.

hantavirus include Russia, Japan, Finland, Sweden, various eastern European countries, and Greece.

Over the course of many years, Swedish researchers have discovered an endemic form of hantavirus disease, which they call nephropathia epidemica. An endemic disease is a disease that is common and always present either at a low or high level in an affected area. The Swedish form of hantavirus infection is caused by the Puumala virus, which was isolated in the 1980s. The animal carrier of the Puumala virus is the bank vole, a mouse-like rodent that lives near rivers and water. The Puumala virus causes the least-deadly known type of HFRS, or the renal syndrome type of hantavirus illness, with a fatality rate of one-tenth of 1 percent. In contrast, the fatality rate for the young, healthy people infected in the Four Corners area was more than 60 percent. The kidney ailments associated with HFRS are typical of Eastern Hemisphere hantavirus illnesses, rather than the pulmonary complaints associated with Western Hemisphere hantavirus.

Before 1996, medical researchers believed that hantavirus-based illness was transmitted only through animal-to-human contact—specifically through people coming into contact with the saliva, urine, or solid waste of rodents. In 1996, however, a new form of hantavirus was discovered in the Rio Negro province of Argentina, which is located in the southern Andes Mountains. The new strain was named the Andes virus. Eighteen people fell ill, exhibiting many symptoms of HPS. Several people who visited the infected patients in the hospital also came down with the illness within three weeks. It is possible that these close friends and family members were exposed to the same rodents that presumably infected the patients. Yet, when three doctors who treated the patients also fell ill, a more disturbing conclusion was reached. The Andes virus appears to be the first known case of hantavirus illness that can be contracted through person-to-person, not animal-to-person, contact.

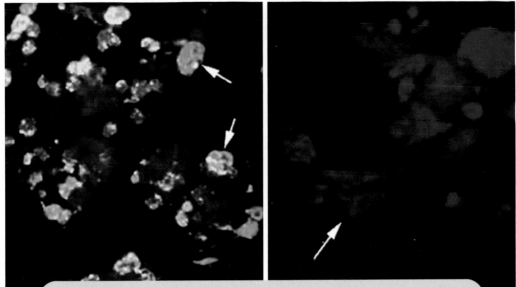

The image on the left shows the blood of a Chilean patient infected with hantavirus. The arrows point to hantavirus antigens—proteins that provoke an immune response against the invading virus. The arrow on the right also points to cells infected by hantavirus, but in which no antigens have yet appeared.

Other hantavirus infections in South America and Central America include an outbreak in the late summer and early fall of 1997 in southern Chile, in which twenty-five people fell ill. It was eventually found to be the same Andes virus that had caused the earlier outbreak in Argentina. A 1999 outbreak in Panama killed three of the twelve people infected. While most of the patients in Panama suffered from HPS, a few suffered from the renal syndrome that is more typical of the Eastern Hemisphere–based hantavirus infections.

Scientists have even come to believe that the "sweating sickness," which spread through London and the English countryside repeatedly during the fifteenth- and sixteenth-century reigns of King Henry VIII and Elizabeth I, was a form of hantavirus. The often fatal illness, which first occurred in 1485 and returned four times over the next century, fit the profile for HPS. The so-called sweating sickness arrived suddenly with fever, profuse sweating, headaches, and extreme shortness of breath. A contemporary English writer claimed that the sickness killed some of its victims within two to three hours. Those who seemed healthy and happy at lunch could be dead by dinnertime.

With the release of each new study on historic outbreaks of the disease and the appearance of new cases of illness, scientists have learned more about how hantavirus is spread, how infections can be treated, and, most important, how to prevent infection in the first place.

3

THE SCIENCE OF EPIDEMIOLOGY

The science of epidemiology—the study of infectious diseases in an entire population rather than on an individual level—really began in the eighteenth century in Europe, the so-called Age of Enlightenment. Just as many other sciences, such as physics, chemistry, and astronomy, were advancing during this time, so too was the study of disease.

Dr. John Snow and the Study of Cholera

One early pioneer of epidemiology was Dr. John Snow, a nineteenth-century British physician. One of the many diseases that regularly afflicted great cities like London was cholera, a disease that is still common today in various parts of the world that suffer from poor hygiene and inadequate sanitation. Cholera is an intestinal disease that causes severe and potentially fatal diarrhea, dehydration, and fever. It is caused by the bacteria *Vibrio cholerae*, which is spread through human excrement (solid waste).

Dr. John Snow, seen above in an 1857 photograph, was a medical pioneer. Along with helping discover the causes of cholera, he was one of the first physicians to promote the use of anesthesia.

In the summer of 1854, Dr. Snow did not know about the existence of bacteria, although he suspected there was an infectious cause to the diseases that seemed to spread without warning throughout the crowded city of London. That summer, a terrible epidemic of cholera raged through the Soho district of the city. Dr. Snow lived nearby and immediately suspected that the source of infection was the water drawn from the public pump located in Broad Street and used by thousands of local residents. Within ten days after the first case occurred, more than 620 people had died of cholera.

Without modern tools, such as a microscope that would allow him to see the cholera bacteria, Dr. Snow set up a geographical grid pinpointing the location of each cholera infection. Using this map of the disease outbreak, he was able to trace each infection back to the water pump. Equally important, Dr. Snow discovered that nearby businesses and residences that did not use water from the pump remained cholera free. Taking his research to city officials, Dr. Snow convinced the skeptical men to take the handle off the pump as an experiment. With this sudden halt to the neighborhood's supply of water, new cholera infections also stopped.

However, town officials were still skeptical of Dr. Snow's theories, in particular his claim that human waste was contaminating the pump water and somehow causing the disease. Dr. Snow himself could not find a direct cause for sewage entering the pump water. In an ironic coincidence, the true cause of the infection was unearthed by one of Dr. Snow's opponents, a local minister who believed that the cholera epidemic was simply God's will. In the course of the minister's investigation of the cholera outbreak, a local woman admitted to washing a sick baby's diaper at the pump and dumping the soiled water only three feet (0.91 meters) from the basin of the water pump in the days before the epidemic began. The dirty diaper seems to have caused the deaths of more than 600 Londoners.

Sadly, however, for a number of years afterward, town officials continued to refuse to believe that there was any connection between poor hygiene and sanitation and outbreaks of dreadful diseases like cholera. Despite Dr. Snow's efforts, the Broad Street pump was not shut down permanently until decades later. It was not until 1893—almost forty years after the formulation of Dr. Snow's pioneering theories on the links between bacteria, infection, and disease—that a German scientist, Dr. Robert Koch, isolated the cholera bacteria and proved that the disease was not passed from person to person, like a cold or the flu. Instead, contact with infected water is what spreads the disease. Therefore, outbreaks can be prevented by proper sanitation.

Although we enjoy safe sanitation in the United States and western Europe today, much of the rest of the world is not so lucky. Sadly, according to the World Health Organization (WHO), cholera infected almost 150,000 people worldwide in 2001, mostly in Africa, and killed almost 5,000.

The Germ Theory of Disease

In the 1880s, Dr. Robert Koch (1843–1910) and Dr. Louis Pasteur (1822–1895; the inventor and namesake of the technique of safe food production called pasteurization) developed the germ theory of disease. At this time, people still believed in many different nongerm causes of disease. Dr. Koch invented a series of postulates, or theories to be tested, that were designed to help physicians and scientists decide whether a disease was caused by infection or some other cause, such as poison or internal illness. In order to determine that a disease has been caused by infection with a bacterial agent, Koch stated that the following must occur:

Dr. Robert Koch, shown here in his laboratory, used the principles of germ theory to make his most famous discovery—identifying the bacteria that caused tuberculosis.

- ✪ The agent must be present in every case of the disease.

- ✪ The agent must be isolated from the host and grown in vitro (outside the living body in an artificial environment, such as a laboratory).

⊛ The disease must be reproduced when a pure culture of the agent is inoculated (introduced or implanted) into a healthy host.

⊛ The same agent must be recovered once again from the experimentally infected host.

In other words, in order to prove that a disease is a result of bacterial infection, Koch stated, the bacteria must be present in every person who has become ill. Doctors have to be able to isolate and remove a sample of the bacteria from an infected person and grow it outside the body in a lab. When this sample bacteria is then introduced to a healthy host—an animal or human—the host must become ill. Finally, the disease-causing bacteria must then be found in the infected host and a sample of it removed for testing. Only when all these conditions were met could doctors be confident that a bacterial infection was at the root of a disease outbreak.

The Differences Between Viruses and Bacteria

Unlike cholera, which is caused by bacteria, hantavirus is caused by a virus, a much smaller infectious agent. Bacteria are extremely tiny, single-celled living organisms that can infect humans, plants, or animals and that often cause disease. Viruses, in contrast, are intercellular parasites, meaning that, unlike bacteria, they cannot survive on their own but rely on hosts to sustain them. They infect living hosts and reside in the hosts' living cells but are not themselves considered to be complete living organisms. Viruses cannot even directly reproduce themselves. A related, much more poorly understood infectious agent is called a prion. Prions are even smaller and more basic than viruses. They are the agents believed to cause mad cow disease (or bovine spongiform encephalopathy) in cows and the related Creutzfeldt-Jakob disease in humans.

Early epidemiologists and doctors like John Snow did not recognize the difference between viruses and bacteria. They just knew that something caused disease and infection, and they suspected it was some type of living particle. Evidence of viral illnesses such as smallpox and poliomyelitis (polio) has been found in Egyptian mummies and illustrated in carvings and reliefs as early as 3700 BC. In these cases, of course, people were very familiar with the telltale symptoms of these diseases but had many mostly incorrect theories as to their causes. The term "virus" was first used in the Middle Ages to describe a slimy, poisonous, or foul-smelling liquid. By the late 1930s, scientists were regularly using the term "filterable virus" to describe those agents capable of passing through filters that were fine enough to catch bacteria.

Vaccination

As early as 1000 BC, a practice called variolation was in use in China. Chinese physicians instructed patients to inhale the dried and ground remains of smallpox lesions taken from smallpox survivors. This was a sort of precursor to the pioneering work performed by Edward Jenner, an eighteenth-century doctor. In 1796, Dr. Jenner inoculated a young boy against the deadly disease smallpox by deliberately infecting him with material from a pox—or runny sore—taken from a milkmaid infected by a similar but much milder disease called cowpox. Dr. Jenner had noticed that milkmaids often became ill with the mild cowpox disease but rarely got the often-deadly and disfiguring disease of smallpox. To test whether infection with cowpox protected against infection with smallpox, Dr. Jenner later infected the boy with real smallpox. Sure enough, the boy did not get the much more dangerous disease. Thus, the science of inoculation, or vaccination (named after the cowpox virus—vaccinia), was begun.

Scientists first began to study the physical properties of viruses in the 1930s with the help of a filtration process that isolated the still poorly understood and unseen agents. Later, more sophisticated instruments used ultraviolet and ordinary light to study viruses. After the development of the first electron microscope in 1931, viruses could be visually studied for the first time. It would not be until 1940, however, that virus particles were actually captured on film and ordinary people could see for themselves that viruses did indeed exist.

By the 1970s, the science of virology had increased in sophistication to the point where the WHO was able to launch a bold plan. Although Edward Jenner had conducted the first vaccination against a viral illness in 1796, the disease of smallpox was still a terrifying worldwide killer. By launching

This nineteenth-century illustration shows Edward Jenner inoculating James Phipps against smallpox with cowpox germs in 1796.

a worldwide vaccination campaign, the WHO was able to officially eliminate smallpox from the world in 1977.

4

HANTAVIRUS CARRIERS, SYMPTOMS, AND PREVENTION

Hantavirus is transmitted through the saliva, urine, and feces of rodents, so prevention of the disease primarily involves developing an awareness of the animal carriers of hantavirus, knowing where they live, and creating and maintaining clean and sterilized living spaces.

Rodent Carriers

When scientists deal with viruses that reside in animal hosts and are then transmitted to the human population, they refer to the animal population as a "reservoir." Although several different species of animals can carry a virus, generally one species is associated with a particular strain of that virus. The deer mouse, for example, is the primary carrier or reservoir of the Sin Nombre strain of hantavirus. Trapping and testing has shown that, on average, about 10 percent of deer mice are infected with hantavirus. The animal itself is not made sick by the virus, but it "sheds" the virus in its urine, saliva, and feces, thus creating the circumstances for potential human infection. Unlike other rodent-associated illnesses like bubonic plague, hantavirus is not vector-borne. A vector-borne illness is transmitted through an insect host—such as a flea or mosquito—that bites a human and injects the infecting microbe directly

A deer mouse nurses her litter in her nest. Deer mice can have up to four litters a year. Although deer mice can be found in people's houses, their natural habitat is inside hollow trees.

into the bloodstream. Instead, hantavirus is contracted through inhalation (breathing in) of or direct contact with infected rodent urine, feces, or saliva.

The most common carrier of the Sin Nombre strain of hantavirus (which is the most common as well as the most dangerous strain of hantavirus in North America) is the deer mouse. The two- to three-inch-long (5- to 7.6-centimeter) deer mouse is found throughout North America and northern Mexico, with the exception of the eastern seaboard and the extreme southern United States. The deer mouse usually lives in wilderness areas, but when its population increases, it is happy to come into the homes of people who live nearby. Its belly is always white, and it has well-defined white sides on its tail, although the rest of its fur can vary from brown to red or gray.

In this 1997 photo, workers build an experimental "rodent reservation" south of Albuquerque, New Mexico, to study hantavirus carriers.

The cotton rat and rice rat are two other Sin Nombre carriers. They are found in the southeastern United States and parts of Central and South America. The cotton rat's body is between five and seven inches long (13 and 18 cm), its fur is somewhat long and coarse, with a grayish brown or grayish black color. It lives in marshy and grassy areas. The rice rat is a little bit smaller than the cotton rat. It has white feet and fur that is softer and grayer than that of the cotton rat. Its tail is longer than its body, and it likes even marshier areas than the cotton rat does.

The white-footed mouse is very similar to the deer mouse. It lives in areas of the United States that the deer mouse does not generally occupy, but it can sometimes be found in western states, as well. Rodents that carry hantavirus are usually found in rural areas, but people should be aware that the deer mouse and the white-footed mouse will enter homes in suburban areas, too.

Before coming down with symptoms of the disease, many people who have contracted HPS cleaned out garages, woodpiles, or areas of their homes that were infested by rats and mice. In doing so, they came into contact with the saliva, urine, and/or feces of the infected rodents and became infected themselves. One victim in the 1993 Four Corners outbreak slept on a couch that was also home to many deer mice.

Hantavirus Phases and Symptoms

Most infectious diseases follow a three-part progression: prodrome (a period of early symptoms of disease), active illness, and the recovery phase. Because hantavirus infection may incubate (develop) in a person's body for one to five weeks before any type of symptoms occur, it is very difficult to detect, diagnose, and treat the illness quickly, before the patient gets very sick.

The HPS prodrome lasts from three to five days and includes fever, chills, and body aches and pains. Other symptoms can include headache, nausea and vomiting, abdominal pain, diarrhea, and a cough. Some patients who contract HPS also report having shortness of breath, dizziness, back or chest pain, and excessive sweating. Medical exams reveal rapid breathing and heartbeat, as well as fever.

Blood platelets are flattened disks in the blood that help in clotting. In about 80 percent of patients who develop HPS, the blood platelet level falls below 150,000 microliters. A sudden fall in blood platelets often signals the transition from the prodrome phase to active illness: the pulmonary edema phase. Pulmonary edema is a condition in which the lungs fill with fluid. It is the most dangerous illness associated with HPS.

During the pulmonary edema phase of HPS, patients develop hypotension, or low blood pressure, as well as hypoxia—oxygen starvation in the body's tissues. Meanwhile the edema worsens so that all parts of the lungs begin to fill with fluid, including the alveoli, which are the sacs in our lungs that allow us to absorb oxygen into our bloodstream. Current intensive care treatment tries to address all three of these conditions (edema, hypotension, and hypoxia) using every method available. Even with this intensive treatment, however, HPS is fatal in about 50 percent of the cases. The earlier patients are admitted for treatment, the more successful treatment is.

One reason patients can become so ill before being diagnosed with hantavirus and HPS is that the virus is very difficult to detect in the blood. So when symptoms seem to indicate HPS, tests are conducted that are designed to detect hantavirus antibodies. Antibodies are proteins that the body produces when a foreign agent, such as a virus, has invaded. When a blood test indicates the presence of hantavirus antibodies, doctors can be sure that the patient has indeed been infected with a hantavirus and thus treat him or her accordingly.

There is no medical cure for hantavirus pulmonary syndrome. There are some treatments that have been developed, but they are palliative, which means they treat symptoms, not the underlying infection causing the illness. However, physicians have been experimenting with new antiviral drugs that would attack the virus directly and hopefully kill it before HPS and other harmful hantavirus symptoms can develop. Patients who do begin to show signs of HPS, however, should be hospitalized immediately. Treatment includes oxygen therapy, positive pressure ventilation (mechanical assistance with breathing), and careful management of the body's fluids.

Because there is no guaranteed cure, prevention is the key to stopping hantavirus infection. The USAMRIID announced in October 2003 that it had developed an experimental vaccine against hantavirus infection using genetic-engineering techniques.

Precautions

The CDC has drawn up a list of precautions that should be taken in order to prevent hantavirus infection. Though people who live in rural southwestern areas are most at risk, hantavirus infection can occur anywhere in the United States.

Indoor Prevention

- Keep a clean home, especially in the kitchen (wash dishes, clean counters and floor, keep food covered in rodent-proof containers).

- Keep a tight-fitting lid on garbage; discard uneaten pet food at the end of the day.

- Set and keep spring-loaded rodent traps. Place traps in areas where rodents might be entering the home. Set traps perpendicular to baseboards with the bait closest to the baseboard or wall (rodents tend to run along walls and in tight spaces rather than out in the open). Use a small amount of chunky peanut butter as bait. Handle traps with caution, and keep children and pets away from the traps.

⊛ Set Environmental Protection Agency–approved rodenti-cide (poison) with bait under plywood or plastic shelter along baseboards. These are sometimes known as covered bait stations. Remember to follow product use instruc-tions carefully, since rodenticides are poisonous to pets and people, too.

Spring-loaded traps can be an effective way to kill rats or mice infesting your home, but be sure to handle the dead animal carefully.

⊛ Seal all entry holes in walls and floors that are ¼ inch (64 mm) wide or wider with lath screen or lath metal, cement, wire screening, or other patching materials, inside and out.

Outdoor Prevention

⊛ Clear brush, grass, and junk from around house foundations to eliminate potential sources of nesting materials.

Store grains and animal feed in rodent-proof containers.

⊛ Use metal flashing around the base of wooden, earthen, or adobe homes to provide a strong metal barrier that will prevent rodent entry into the house. Install the flashing so that it reaches 12 inches (30 cm) above the ground and 6 inches (15 cm) down into the ground.

Store hay, woodpiles, and garbage cans off the ground in order to eliminate possible nesting sites. If possible, locate them 100 feet (30 m) or more from your house.

⊛ Set outdoor traps for rodents. Poisons or rodenticides may also be used, but be sure to keep them out of the reach of playing children and pets.

⊛ Encourage the presence of natural predators, such as nonpoisonous snakes, owls, and hawks.

The Role of Ecology, Climate, and Tradition

The 1993 Four Corners outbreak showed how ecologists and climatologists could work together to play an important part in understanding and helping prevent disease. The chances of hantavirus infection in humans directly increase in relation to the number of infected animals that live near people. Some animals that carry the virus are not serious threats to human populations, since they live in such remote areas and their numbers are so small that people seldom, if ever, come into contact with them.

This is not the case with the deer mouse. Ecologists and climatologists found that the winter of 1992 was the wettest in many years in the American Southwest because of the El Niño weather phenomenon off the Pacific coast. This unusual moisture caused a huge increase in the piñon (pine) nut crop, the deer mouse's favorite food supply. As a result, the deer mouse population increased dramatically. Because there was suddenly such a large number of deer mice, they began to spread beyond their usual habitations to search for more food and living space. They began to move ever closer to human populations in the Four Corners area. By 1993, the conditions were ripe for a tragic outbreak of hantavirus.

Studies on the local deer mouse population and how it was affected by climate change were available to the scientists studying the 1993 outbreak thanks to data provided by the Sevilleta Long Term Ecological Research program (LTER) funded by the National Science Foundation. In addition, museum samples collected by the LTER study team over a period of time showed that the Sin Nombre virus was present in rodents before the 1993 outbreak. Although the deer mouse population normally has a hantavirus infection rate of 10 percent, CDC epidemiologists found that 30 percent of the deer mice they caught near the homes of people who had fallen ill with HPS in 1993 were infected with the Sin Nombre virus. The rapid rodent population growth seemed to have caused increased amounts of hantavirus infection.

The research teams that investigated the 1993 outbreak also found that some Navajo elders had predicted the situation. *Navajo Lifeways: Contemporary Issues, Ancient Knowledge*, by researcher Maureen Trudelle Schwarz, records statements made by Navajo elders about the Four Corners epidemic. The elders consider mice to be "bearers of illness from ancient times if the two worlds mingle." A Navajo medicine man stated, "We didn't have to wait for scientists to tell us what happened . . . We brought it upon ourselves" by not following the teachings of the Holy People.

Though elders had noticed the heavy winter rains and the resulting increase in mouse populations, they did not raise any alarm or remind their people of traditional ways to prevent rodent-borne illnesses. Traditionally, Navajo healers have taught their people that the presence of mice in homes increased the risk of infection and illness because of contact with mouse droppings and urine. The illness was thought to enter through the mouth, nose, or eyes, and it usually attacked the strongest and healthiest of the Navajo people. Traditional Navajo medicine prescribed avoiding mice, keeping them out of the hogans (Navajo homes), and isolating and protecting food supplies. So, while Western medicine and science thought the Sin Nombre virus was causing a new and terrifying disease, Navajos had known of the killing power of the hantavirus for many generations.

A combination of this ancient wisdom and the development of modern vaccines may finally provide a way to prevent or even eradicate hantavirus infection in the future.

5

BIOTERRORISM AND THE FUTURE OF HANTAVIRUS

In the post–September 11 world, in which fear of terrorist attacks of all sorts preoccupies much of the Western world, the threat of bioterrorism (the use of potentially deadly infectious agents as weapons on civilian and military populations) has received growing attention. Bioterrorism was initially feared as a potential cause of the 1993 Four Corners outbreak of hantavirus, but its true cause was ultimately found to be weather changes that caused an explosion in the deer mouse population and its rate of hantavirus infection. Some scientists also feared bioterrorism as a potential cause of the Ebola epidemics in Africa beginning in the 1970s. Ebola causes a highly deadly hemorrhagic fever. The thought that this type of disease could be used as a weapon against innocent people is truly terrifying.

Many countries, including the United States, have investigated the possibility of using infectious diseases as weapons. Weaponization, or turning a disease from a microbe into a deadly weapon, involves many complicated steps. Not all diseases can be weaponized, and some are more easily weaponized than others. The history of using disease as a weapon is long.

The Pulitzer Prize–winning book *Guns, Germs, and Steel* (1997), by California biologist Jared Diamond, argues that western European resistance to many serious "crowd" diseases, such as measles and smallpox, played an important part in the European domination of the New World as well as other parts of the world. Diseases brought by Europeans shrank Native American populations to a fraction of their former levels within a century of European arrival. Germs, not guns, provided the European victory over native peoples. In some cases, the use of germs as a weapon was quite intentional. For example, American settlers distributed measles- and smallpox-infected blankets to Native Americans during territorial wars with various tribes.

Happily, the United States' research into the offensive use of bioweapons has ceased. In the 1970s, while

This child shows the characteristic lesions of smallpox, a disease now so rare that most doctors have never seen a case of it. Routine vaccination of children against smallpox in the United States stopped in 1972, because the disease was eliminated and the vaccine itself posed a small risk of giving children smallpox.

other countries continued to develop biological weapons in secret, the United States' offensive bioweapons program was eliminated, and its resources, labs, and scientists were redirected to research into cures and prevention in the case of biological attack.

One of the most feared potential bioweapons is smallpox because it is so infectious. Although officials state that there are only two remaining collections of the smallpox virus located in secure freezers in the United States and Russia, terrorist fears have raised alarms that these supplies could be stolen and turned into weapons. The bioweapons program of the former

Soviet Union was particularly active, and former Soviet bioweapons scientists who now live and work in the United States have described the development of thousands of liters of infectious smallpox in weapons labs. Today, the United States is working hard to create enough vaccine to stop any smallpox bioattack on its people or soldiers at home and abroad. Health and safety workers—like doctors, nurses, and disease researchers—and many military personnel have already received their vaccinations.

Like many of the most feared and deadly viruses, including Lassa, Ebola, and Marburg fevers, the hantavirus is a hemorrhagic fever. All hemorrhagic fevers can be turned into weapons. What would be necessary to turn hantavirus into a biological weapon? First, scientists employed by terrorists or rogue states would probably have to manipulate the virus's genetic code in order to increase its rate of infection. Right now, many more people are exposed to hantavirus than actually end up coming down with the disease. In addition, some healthy people test positive for hantavirus antibodies, which means they have been infected, but they show no symptoms. For the virus to be effective as a weapon, it would have to cause high rates of infection.

Currently, the most likely use for hantavirus as a weapon would be similar to the anthrax attack of fall 2001 in the United States. In this attack, a still-unidentified terrorist sent powdered anthrax—a powerfully toxic, spore-forming bacterium—through the mail. Several individuals who received and opened envelopes containing the powdery substance were killed, several more became seriously ill, and many government buildings, network television offices, and post offices were contaminated and temporarily closed. However, unlike anthrax, which is easily grown and produced in a laboratory environment, hantavirus cannot be so easily grown.

Because of the risk U.S. military personnel face of contracting HFRS while stationed in Korea, the USAMRIID has developed a vaccine that has produced a strong immune response in animals that were infected with hantavirus. It is already in experimental use. Because of its special expertise in hantavirus outbreaks, the USAMRIID worked closely with national, state, and local health agencies during the 1993 Four Corners outbreak. The USAMRIID is just one office of the Defense Department's scientific and medical command devoted to the fight against infectious diseases, and it continues to play an important role in the research and development of vaccines, treatments, and cures that can help everyone around the world remain healthy.

An ancient killer that took modern medicine by surprise during the Four Corners outbreak in 1993, hantavirus inspires both fascination and fear. Through a combination of education, research, prevention, treatment, and, perhaps someday soon, vaccination, hantavirus should not continue to be a fatal disease. Many different groups of physicians, scientists, and ordinary people are working to understand and fight the hantavirus. The combination of time-honored Navajo wisdom and the most current laboratory techniques mean that the "killer that steals babies' breath" will not likely be able to continue its silent stalking in years to come.

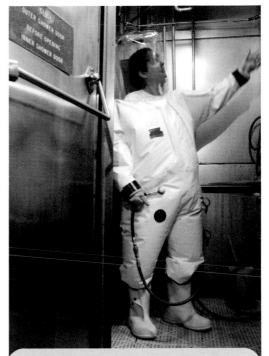

Dr. Catherine Wilhemson, biosecurity manager for USAMRIID, demonstrates a decontamination room during a tour of the USAMRIID Patient Containment Lab in 2004.

GLOSSARY

bacterium (plural: bacteria) A single-celled living organism, considered the simplest form of complete life.

bioterrorism The use of biological infectious agents to harm and terrorize innocent people.

DNA Short for deoxyribonucleic acid, it is the basic form of genetic material that guides the development of life.

edema The condition of being physically swollen with fluid.

epidemiology The study of population-level causes and effects of infectious disease.

hemorrhagic Resulting in massive, difficult-to-control bleeding.

platelets Circulating blood cells that are crucial to the process of clotting.

pulmonary Referring to the lungs.

renal Referring to the kidneys.

RNA A type of genetic material, often the basis for virus replication (self-reproduction).

shock A physical state in which circulating blood cannot deliver adequate oxygen to vital organs.

virus A microscopic organism that contains genetic material but that cannot replicate outside of a living cell.

FOR MORE INFORMATION

In the United States

American Lung Association
61 Broadway, 6th Floor
New York, NY 10006
(212) 315-8700 or (800) LUNG-USA
Web site: http://www.lungusa.org

Centers for Disease Control and
  Prevention (CDC)
National Center for Infectious
  Diseases (NCID)
1600 Clifton Road
Atlanta, GA 30333
(404) 639-3311 or (800) 311-3435
Web site: http://www.cdc.gov/ncidod

Federation of American Societies for
  Experimental Biology
9650 Rockville Pike
Bethesda, MD 20814
(301) 634-7000
Web site: http://www.faseb.org

National Institute of Allergy and Infectious Diseases
6610 Rockledge Drive, MSC 6612
Bethesda, MD 20872-6612
Web site: http://www.niaid.nih.gov/default.htm

National Institutes of Health (NIH)
9000 Rockville Pike
Bethesda, MD 20892
(301) 496-4000
Web site: http://www.nih.gov

U.S. National Library of Medicine
8600 Rockville Pike
Bethesda, MD 20894
Web site: http://www.nlm.nih.gov

World Health Organization (WHO)
525 23rd Street NW
Washington, DC 20037
(202) 974-3000
Web site: http://www.who.int/en

In Canada

Health Canada
A.L. 0900C2
Ottawa, Ontario K1A 0K9
(613) 957-2991 or (800) 267-1245
Web site: http://www.hc-sc.gc.ca/english

Web Sites

Due to the changing nature of Internet links, the Rosen Publishing Group, Inc., has developed an online list of Web sites related to the subject of this book. This site is updated regularly. Please use this link to access the list:

http://www.rosenlinks.com/epid/hant

FOR FURTHER READING

De Kruif, Paul, and F. Gonzales-Cruissi. *Microbe Hunters*. New York: Harvest Books, 2002.

Desalle, Rob, ed. *Epidemic! The World of Infectious Disease*. New York: New Press, 1999.

Hyde, Margaret O., and Elizabeth H. Forsyth, MD. *Vaccinations: From Smallpox to Cancer*. New York: Franklin Watts, 2000.

Jakab, E. A. M. *Louis Pasteur: Hunting Killer Germs*. New York: McGraw Hill/Contemporary Books, 2000.

Nardo, Don. *Germs*. San Diego: Kidhaven, 2001.

Nardo, Don. *Vaccines*. San Diego: Lucent Books, 2001.

Peters, C. J., and Mark Olshaker. *Virus Hunter: Thirty Years of Battling Hot Viruses Around the World*. New York: Anchor, 1998.

BIBLIOGRAPHY

CDC.gov. "All About Hantaviruses." June 2004. Retrieved August 2004 (http://www.cdc.gov/ ncidod/diseases/hanta/hps/noframes/outbreak. htm).

Diamond, Jared. *Guns, Germs, and Steel*. New York: W. W. Norton, 1993.

Handelman, Stephen, and Ken Alibek. *Biohazard: The Chilling True Story of the Largest Covert Biological Weapons Program in the World—Told from Inside by the Man Who Ran It*. New York: Delta, 2000.

Harper, David, and Andrea Meyer. *Of Mice, Men, and Microbes: Hantavirus*. San Diego: Academic Press, 1999.

McCormick, Joseph. *Level 4: Virus Hunters of the CDC*. Nashville: Turner Publishing Company, 1996.

Preston, Richard. *The Demon in the Freezer*. New
York: Fawcett, 2003.

Preston, Richard. *The Hot Zone*. New York:
Anchor, 1995.

Rang, Lee Wha. "Japan's Germ Warfare and the
Korean War." Korea Web Weekly, July 27, 1996.
Retrieved August 2004 (http://www.kimsoft.com/
korea/jp-germ.htm).

Schwarz, Maureen Trudelle. *Navajo Lifeways:
Contemporary Issues, Ancient Knowledge*. Tulsa,
OK: University of Oklahoma Press, 2001.

INDEX

CREDITS

About the Author

Amy Sterling Casil is a freelance author living in California.

Photo Credits